Power 2 Go:

A Prayer Manuel

Okisha L Jackson

asf.bookseries@aol.com

www.twitter.com/SheNevaStuck

All Scripture quotations are from the Message Bible, NLT, and the King James Version of the Bible.

Influence of prayers comes from the Holy Ghost, Dr. Cindy Trimm's book The Rules of Engagement, the book Prayers by Christian Word Ministries from Lexington Kentucky, and Prayers that Break Curses by John Eckhardt,

Printing by CreateSpace, An Amazon.com Company

Book Formatting by EbookLaunch

Editing by Okisha Jackson

Cover Design created by EbookLaunch

Power 2 Go: A Prayer Manuel/ Okisha Jackson. — 1st Ed.

ISBN 13: 978-1540698957

Dedications

Alice B. Walton-Ramsey
December 3, 1933 to September 1990

To my beloved Grandma. You were the first person who ever taught me how to pray. You planted the first seed introducing me to the Lord's Prayer in Matthew chapter 6 and now God uses me to write for his glory. I look forward to seeing you after I close my eyes for the last time grandma. Thank you so much. I love and miss you.

Maryellen Meredith Crockett

To the truest and realest spiritual mother and prayer warrior that I have ever known Glory to God. Thank you for obeying the Holy Spirit as He led you to ask me to start praying. That was over twelve years ago. Can you believe it? Look what God has done! I thank God for you and all you have imparted into me throughout the years. I can't thank you and dad enough. I look forward to the day we all can shout and run around the church together. Love you and dad, Pastor Howard A. Crockett, forever.

Table of Contents

Introduction

Greetings Readers,

This book is a handy tool the Spirit of the Lord told me to create for people like me. As a single mom of three boys, a caretaker to my mother, a part-time teacher, minister, and as you can see, writer, I am always on the go. I need a little prayer book that's quick and powerful as I go on my way.

This book will not be long, but I must advise you. These prayers are the ones that require a lifestyle that's committed to God daily with praying and fasting. These will not be surface or "cute" prayers.

This is for **Prayer Warriors**.

Prayer warriors know that Satan, our adversary, is a legalist, a liar, and a thief; the list goes on. However, the Lord Jesus, our chief intercessor, and the Holy Spirit has taught me how to war in ways I didn't know we could. The Lord is very strategic. He has given us a lot of authority that we don't even know we have. I know this book will help you. Are you ready to kick some devil butt? Good. People of God it's on. Let's go!

Initial Prayer

Lord Jesus, I lift up everyone that will get this book and everyone they will pray for, that we all would be full of the Holy Ghost like your disciple Stephen who was the first martyr in the book of Acts.

I ask that all of us are hidden and protected from all demonic counter attacks from the kingdom of darkness, all sins committed by our relatives, and every prayer prayed is submerged in the blood of Jesus Christ.

I pray and ask that every prayer prayed from the heart with sincerity is answered immediately and the blood of Jesus rebukes all delays of all kinds from our prayers being answered in the name of Jesus Christ of Nazareth.

I secure every prayer and every person that utilizes this book with the insurance of Psalm 91: 1-16, Job 1: 7-10, and the entire Psalm of 121 in Jesus name we pray and seal these things in the blood of Jesus right now Lord according to John 16:23 Amen and Amen.

Wake Down

Our Father which art in Heaven, hollowed be thy name. Thank you for waking me up this morning. I come down now on my knees repenting before I ask you for anything.

Before I go any further, I ask you Jesus Christ of Nazareth to bind satan, all demonic intel and network, all demonic surveillance, and the enemies of my own soul and the souls of those I will be in the midst of today, their eyes blind and their ears deaf to my prayers, conversations, and actions right now, throughout this day and night.

Please forgive me Father for all my sins. For disobedience and rebellion. For taking your kindness for weakness and your grace for granted. Please cleanse me from my secret faults, presumptuous sins, and perfect those things which concerns me.

Please give me true humility, Godly-sorrow, and a stronger conviction against sin. Forgive me Holy Spirit for defiling and grieving you. Please enable me to honor and respect you the way you deserve to be.

Jesus please have mercy on me, a sinner, I re-dedicate my life to you. Please be the ruler, Lord, and the head of my entire being. Lord Jesus please cast out every idol I've placed over you and sever every curse, word curses, all strongholds and hindrances, all demonic contaminations I opened the door to.

In Jesus name I pray and ask you Heavenly Father according to John 16:23 and I seal this prayer in the blood of Jesus Christ your son and ask that it be answered immediately by the power, anointing, and effects of your holy word, the Bible, has had on bringing your children back home from the day of its origination even until now amen.

Get Clean

Holy Spirit Good Morning, I ask you to please pray with me and through me because I can't out pray you.

Father God in heaven we come to you in the name of your son Jesus Christ of Nazareth and we ask you to bind and loose from us all demonic host, principalities, ruler of wickedness in high places, all generational curses, everything we've contracted in the spiritual realm that's demonic from dreams, visions, imaginations, soulish attacks, and all of their effects, adverse effects, stings, wrong mind sets that's come in us, about us and in the heavens completely.

We ask you to bind and loose from us everything written in Mark 7:21&22, Ephesians 4:31, 1 Corinthians 6:9&10, Galatians 5:19, 20, & 21, 2 Timothy 3:2-5, Romans 1:29-32, and every spot, blemish, and wrinkle on our robes that would keep us from inheriting your kingdom if you should take us home today.

We send all these spears, barbs, chains, wires, links, fruits, roots, all attachments and devices of all kind, and tentacles from us and send them straight to the pit of hell with no replacements. And place the blood of the Lord Jesus Christs and the fire of the Holy Ghost between us and them right now, throughout this day all the way until tomorrow night in the name of Jesus Christ of Nazareth.

We ask you Heavenly Father according to John 16:23 to seal this entire prayer, our deliverances, the signs, symptoms, and manifestations of our deliverances in the blood of Jesus Christ of Nazareth right now please amen and amen.

Suit Up

Jesus, our chief intercessor, we thank you for making provisions for us to have a suit of amour. We put on the whole amour of God that's written in Ephesians 6:10-18.

We put on the **helmet of salvation** and encase it with the power and anointing of psalm 19:1-14 to be a strong buffer against all darts and vain imaginations.

We put on the **breastplate of righteousness** and encase it with the power and anointing of Jude 1:21 to repel all satanic penetrations.

We put on the **shield of faith** and encase it with the power and anointing of Hebrews 11:1 to attack all unbelief.

We put on the **girdle of truth** and encase it with the power and anointing of 1 Corinthians 9:27 to rebuke all the dictates of the flesh.

We put on our **sandals of peace** and encase it with the power and anointing of Psalm 23:2 that our steps are ordered by you all the day long.

We take hold of our **sword of the spirit** and encase it with the power and anointing of Hebrews

4:12 to be effective warriors for your glory.

We plead the blood of Jesus Christ of Nazareth over our whole armor and pray that it be the maximum level of strength and protection that you know we will need for today in the name of Jesus Christ of Nazareth. We ask you according to John 14:13-14 amen and amen.

Cover

Heavenly Father we come to you in the name of your son Jesus and plead the blood of Jesus over ourselves, loved ones, friends, enemies, our neighbors, co-workers, everyone we come in contact with, and our community.

We plead the blood of Jesus from the top of our heads to the soles of our feet, the atmosphere around, over, and under us.

Our whole amour of God, our coming and going, over the screens of every electronic device we use throughout this day that nothing demonic transfers unto us in any kind of way. Over our Wi-Fi, Bluetooth, internet frequencies, internet activities, connectivity, and our identities.

We plead the blood of Jesus over everything we have and will have, over our witness for you wherever we go so, we don't embarrass your kingdom, every door and window of our homes and vehicles. Over our gates and doors to our souls.

Over our prayers, finances, marriages, properties, cell phone frequencies, car, trucks, and telephone and cell phone lines.

We plead the blood of Jesus over our focus and

concentration, our spiritual discernment, steadfastness in you, our hormones and chemical balances, our tongues, mouths, conversations, communications, and our feelings and emotions throughout this day and night in the name of Jesus Christ of Nazareth we ask according to John 14:13-14 amen and amen.

Protect

Heavenly Father we ask you to be our fence today. We declare Psalm 91 1-16, Exodus 12:13, Job 1:7-10 over us, everyone we've prayed for on today, and every person we will come in contact with throughout this day and night in the name of Jesus.

We loose the power and anointing of these scriptures around us as a shield prohibiting all soulish and demonic attacks, protect us from all the sins of our relatives, all accidents, hurt, harm, retaliation, danger, sickness, illnesses, viruses, diseases, hexes, vexes, curses, incantations, racism, hatred, bigotry, jealousies, word curses, everything that falls under the host of the Cain spirit, demons that follow us, familiar spirits, unrighteous agreements being prayed and spoken about us in the name, and demons that are answering wrong prayers about us in the name of Jesus Christ of Nazareth.

We also use these scriptures as a buffer against the enemies of our own souls that we will not be used as tools by the devil in any way in the name of Jesus.

Father God in heaven we ask you to do this right now please in the precious name of your holy son according to John 16:23.

Suicide

Heavenly Father, the Holy Spirit and I come to you in the name of your son Jesus Christ of Nazareth and in the fire and power of the Holy Ghost.

We employ and activate the entire word of Psalms 23, Psalm 93, Psalm 121, and Psalm 91 and the power and anointing of them all to be our steel of protection all around us, over us, under us, as well for our families, friends, neighbors, enemies, and everyone we come into contact with on today.

Please hover your foot over us that it hides us from all supernatural demonic attacks of all kinds and the enemies of our own soul according to Psalm 62:2-3 "**H**ide me from the secret counsel of the wicked; from the insurrection from the workers of iniquity. Who whet their tongue like a sword, and bends their bows to shoot their arrows, even bitter words".

We pray it is our strong buffer and protector against all demonic attacks from all witches and warlocks, all their prayers, charismatic and psychic prayers, hexes, vexes, curses, incantations, chains, fetters, snares, traps, darts, plots, ploys, and plans, demonic strongholds, spells, witchcraft spells, voodoo spells, black magic spells, white magic spells, false prophecies, and word curses.

In the name of Jesus Christ of Nazareth every one of their attacks is returned to sender and an automatic evaporation of their existence never to be replaced.

All of their attacks is an automatic suicide mission and destroys them immediately forever and there can be no demonic counter-attacks against us and this prayer. And they are destroyed like the witches in the Wizard of Oz movie in the name of Jesus Christ of Nazareth we pray and ask you Heavenly Father according to John 14:13-14. And we seal, end, and cover this prayer in the blood of Jesus your son amen and amen.

Focus

Heavenly Father we need your help right now. We pray for you to anoint our eyes, mind, thinking patterns to operate according to your optimum divine design.

We trust and take your word as our medicine, our holy pill of volume, to re-align our focus and concentration right now in the name of Jesus Christ of Nazareth.

Be in our breath as we calm our souls down and please down load your instructions and help us to accomplish each task one at a time for the rest of this day.

We ask all these things in the name of Jesus Christ of Nazareth according to John 16:23 amen.

Alert

Heavenly Father, we ask you to help us stay alert no matter how good things may look or seem because our adversary, the devil, is roaming looking to see who he can devour.

Father our world is in a state of emergency, enable us to be aggressive in prayer and in the right position to war for you as you would have us to in the name of Jesus Christ of Nazareth.

By the power of your word, please become our spiritual humidifier, our peppermint oil to awaken our spiritual senses and discernment just as Jesus had when he knew the women with the issue of blood touched his garment and became healed.

Disable all spirits in us of laziness, mind-blocking, hindrances, slothfulness, gluttony, weariness, struggling, heaviness, and luke warmness.

We ask you to do these things for us right now please in the name of our soon coming king, Jesus, according to John 16:23 amen.

Coffee

Heavenly Father, Jesus, you are my daily bread.

You know what we have need of and right now we need your help Lord.

We ask you to give us the energy we need and send the anointing of your word to kidnap our bloodstream and DNA to become our stimulant, our coffee lord in the name of Jesus Christ of Nazareth.

Father God please release a supernatural rush of your power from the Holy Ghost into our system that puts the dependency we have for caffeine to shame like never before so, we can be all that you need us to be for your glory, our families, and everyone who needs us today in the name of Jesus Christ of Nazareth we pray according to John 16:23 amen.

Mission

Father God there are so many distractions out there, we need your help to stay mission minded, to be the light that you called us to be in a dark world Lord in the name of Jesus. Lord, we pray that wherever we go today your power Jesus, you're anointing, your presence would saturate us so much that as we touch people by your leading that shackles and chains would fall off of them immediately.

That someone would be set free from a generational curse, a sickness, a mental disorder, back pain, heart trouble, diabetes, hatred, bitterness, rebellion, the spirit of the anti-Christ, Lucifer, spells, witchcraft prayers, carnal co-dependencies of all sorts, and whatever you know they need Lord in the name of Jesus Christ of Nazareth.

Lord, we ask that when the deliverances takes place there can be no more room for another demonic entity of any sort, only the fire of the Holy Spirit we pray and ask all these things according to John 16:23 amen.

Praise

Heavenly Father you are my **Elohay Tehilati**. The God of My Praise. You told the Israelites to shout after they walked around Jericho seven times and the walls came tumbling down.

Father I thank you for the victories you given me through the years.

I praise you for Jesus, I praise you for the Holy Spirit, I praise you for my parents, I praise you for my kids, I praise you for the giving me tithes and offerings, I praise you for lights on in the house, I praise you for my toothbrush and toothpaste, I praise you for a job to go to, friends to call, a church to call home, I praise you for a car to drive, a roof over my head, and food to eat.

I praise you for waking me this morning, sweet sleep, and the ability to dress myself and do for myself, I bless your holy name, You are everything, You are mightier than the noise of many waters, the issues in my life, You are mightier than waves of the sea forever and ever,

I praise you Father and thank you for breaking down the walls of opposition in my life and my children's life in the name of Jesus Christ Nazareth according to John 14:13-14 amen.

Charge Up

Heavenly Father we come to you right now and charge up our spirits like we do our cell phones when they get too low. Lord Jesus we're on the run and on the go therefore, we need the power of the Holy Ghost to breathe on us as you did your disciples before your ascension.

We employ every Psalm written by your servant King David, that you know we need to be activated in, over, under, and around us as a shield, a portal for your glory, favor, and the abundant life that your son Jesus died for us to have right now in the name of Jesus Christ of Nazareth please.

We ask you Holy Spirit to be our refreshing, our second wind, to send your strong wind into our temples and every place we go.

Then, like a wildfire, Holy Spirit spread out through us, to speak in a number of different languages as you would have us to according to Act 2:3 in the name of Jesus Christ of Nazareth we pray Heavenly Father and ask according to John 14:13-14 amen.

Activate

Heavenly Father in the name of Jesus Christ of Nazareth, we ask you to activate all the gifts, anointing, and warriors that you have created us to be, our loved ones, and everybody we will come in contact with on today.

By the power of the resurrection of your son Jesus, we ask you to resurrect everything that's dead in us that you want active and working in our lives.

Lord Jesus please resurrect our relationship with you, joy, peace, self-control, long suffering, patience, kindness, consideration for others, empathy, compassion, love for purity, love for holiness, love for pleasing you, love for treating one another with respect, and most importantly love for hearing and doing your word and being prayerful.

Lord Jesus activate your desires in us, your will for our lives, and deliver us from spiritual laziness of all kinds we ask according to John 16:23 amen.

Rebuke

Heavenly Father you are bigger than every problem we're facing right now. We lift you up! You are mightier than any and everything the devil tries to throw our way.

We ask you Father God of Heaven by the power you gave your son Jesus to heal and do all the miracles He ministered while he was on this earth to rebuke all signs, symptoms, and manifestations in both realms death, premature death, Satanism, the anti-Christ spirit, the spirit of Lucifer, the spirit of Jezebel and Ahab and their entire kingdom, Apollyon, Python, mind blocking & mind blocking spirits, poverty, dumb and deaf spirits, all addictions and bondages, all self-destructive generational curses, divination, sorcery, spells, hexes, vexes, incantations, demons that follow and track us, word curses, mind confusion, the spirit of fear and rebellion, the spirit of murder and jealousy, the spirit of competition, anxiety and insecurity, self-delusion, self-destructive, sabotage, apathy, vanity, and pride.

From the least of them to the hosts of them all we loose them from us and everybody connected to us spiritually and physically and place the blood of

Jesus Christ between us and everybody we know that's alive. We also place the blood of Jesus over this prayer and rebuke all delays that would come against it, in the name of Jesus Christ of Nazareth we pray and ask all these things according to John 16:23 amen.

Binding & Loosing

Heavenly Father, we bind and loose according to Matthew 18:18 and Matthew 16:19. In this prayer, we include ourselves, our family members, everyone that goes to our church, our communities, schools that are friends and loved ones attend, even strangers that will be within our midst on today.

We bind and loose everything that's on us that's written in the entire word of God, The Bible that would keep us from inheriting your kingdom if you should take us home today.

We bind and loose all their soul ties, cords, powers, works, roots, fruits, tentacles, the day of their origination, residue, spears, barbs, chains, shackles, ties, wires, and devices of all kinds. We ask you Heavenly Father and thank you very much, and we ask all these things to be done according to John 14:13-14 in the name of Jesus Christ of Nazareth we pray amen and amen.

Sentencing

Heavenly Father, we come asking you to be our **Elohay Mishpat**, the God of Justice in the name of Jesus Christ of Nazareth, who sits at your right hand, and is the one that helped makes us into your own image.

We present our petition to you Lord, the righteous judge and ruler to bring vengeance on our behalf and bring us justice.

Lord, according to your word in Psalm 14 it states, "The fool has said in his heart that there is no God," We ask that every demonic spirit, curse, and powers from the least to the greatest levels of existence that has touched your anointed, brought harm to your prophets, answered wrong prayers concerning us, and attacked us in times when were unaware or vulnerable to be fully terminated from their assignments without the ability to be re-assigned another specialty, banned from the planet earth and all humans, sentenced to the pit of hell until their final place in the lake of fire in the name of Jesus Christ of Nazareth.

We plead the blood of Jesus over this prayer and that it rebukes all delays that would come against it, all supernatural counter-attacks from the kingdom of hell, all evils and darkness, and even Satan himself.

We thank you Lord Jesus that it is done and ask you Heavenly Father to do this right now please according to John 16:23 in your son Jesus name we pray amen and amen.

Talking Back

Lord Jesus, you cursed the fig tree and it bore no more fruit because you said so (Mark 11).

So right now we say to all those fig trees of negative words that have been spoken against me and my family that YOU ALL SHALL NOT BEAR ANY FRUIT! All those curses that are entering into the physical realms of our lives are cancelled, destroyed, and annihilated this instant for all eternity in the name of Jesus Christ of Nazareth.

We shake the dust off of our feet of people who cannot accept how and what you've created us to be and we say to the souls of every loose tongue that doesn't fear the Lord God of Heaven if you don't have anything nice to say be safe and don't say nothing at all.

Enable us Jesus to be quick and bold in battle when a word curse comes out of person as an attack against us that's in our presence, when the enemy comes in like a flood, we ask you to take over our tongues to respond, and that your standard and banner be raised up against him like a flood in the name of Jesus Christ of Nazareth we pray and ask according to John 14:13-14 amen and amen.

Taking Back

Holy Spirit we call on you for back up because the kingdom suffereth violence, and the violent take it by force.

Throughout our whole lives the enemy has been stealing so much from us, but today is a new day.

Father God in Heaven, please forgive us for every open door of sins in our lives, we repent in the name of Jesus Christ your son and close those doors and seal them shut with the blood of Jesus.

We rededicate our lives to you Jesus right now, please wash and cleanse our robes from all sins that would keep us out of Heaven if we had to come home today in the name of Jesus according to 1John 1:9.

Now that we're seated in heavenly places with you and our names have been re-written in the lambs book of life, we take back every blessing, favor, protection, gifts, anointing, praise, worship, every promise written in the bible, and the abundant life Jesus Christ suffered and died for us to have right now in the name of Jesus Christ of Nazareth we pray Father God according to John 16:23 amen and amen.

Strength

Heavenly Father, ask you to be our **Elohay Mauzi**, the God of My strength in the name of Jesus Christ your son, The Holy Spirit and I come in agreement to ask you for strength right now according to Isaiah 40:31.

That you would renew our strength and enable us to mount up with wings as eagles as our second wind enabling us to run and not be weary, to keep walking and not faint, and to bear our cross with gratitude because we are not worthy to have one.

Please deliver us from unbelief, heaviness, complaining, whining, bitterness and all of its poison, and turning to unhealthy ways of processing our emotions that's on us from the least to the highest levels of existence because we know that really ticks you off and embarrasses your kingdom. Lord Jesus, our chief intercessor, apostle, and high priest. Please remind us of your promises and give us steadfast faith to hold onto them just like father Abraham did, we ask in your name according to John 14:13-14 amen.

Road Rage

Heavenly Father, please be my **Jehovah Shalom** right now, I thank you for allowing me to have a vehicle to drive, but I/we need your help because we kind of lose it a little bit on the road.

Lord we plead the blood of Jesus over the tires of our vehicles, our reactions and emotions when people cut us off, take our parking spaces that they knew we was waiting for, take forever and a day to make a turn, speed pass us with anger, turn in front of us making us slam on our brakes, people not using their turn signals, not moving when the light turn green, driving too slow because their on the phone or texting, throwing up cussing finger gestures because we doing the right thing, and riding our tail gate because we won't speed up.

Lord Jesus, sometimes most of us want to get out of our cars and kick their behinds, but we know vengeance is yours. Please help us to forgive them quickly and move on so, the enemy don't use this tactic as a means to pull us out of the center of your love that's written in Jude 1:20-21 right now please in Jesus name we ask you Father God in Heaven according to John 16:23 and we ask that this prayer also be applied to the ones who practice these things mentioned in this prayer amen and amen.

Staying on Task

Heavenly Father, we ask you to help us stay on task. Everywhere we have veered away from doing what you know we need to do, please move us right back to your path in the spiritual and natural realms of our lives.

We bind up all host, principalities, demons, and devils of memory loss, forgetfulness, and mind binding spirits, mind blocking spirits, all hindering spirits, spirts of distractions and frustration, spirits of confusion, and the spirits of doubt.

According to Matthew 16 and 18 we loose all these satanic things immediately from us, our minds, souls, feelings, our blood line, hormones and chemical balances in our bodies, our emotions, and our coming and going right now in the name of Jesus and we send them to the pit of hell straight-way and place the blood of the Lord Jesus Christ between us throughout this day all the way until tomorrow evening in Jesus name we pray.

We thank you Lord and plead your blood over this prayer, and ask all these things according to John 16:23 Amen and Amen.

Thank God

Lord, it is the end of the day and we just want to say thank you that you brought us through it. We thank you for protecting us, guiding us, keeping us, and blessing us.

Thank you Lord for answering our prayers that we prayed throughout this day.

Thank you for opening doors and opportunities for us.

Thank you for blocking us from things and people that mean us no good.

Thank you for being our Shepard, our shade at our right hand, and our helper according to Psalm 121.

Thank you God that even when things didn't go our way in certain areas of our lives you're still faithful and sovereign.

Thank you God the Father, God the Son, and God the Holy Spirit.

Repent

Heavenly Father, please be my **Elohay Selichot** , my God of forgiveness in the name of your son Jesus. Please forgive me for my sins, transgressions, iniquities, sins of commission and omission, sins of disobedience and rebellion, sins that I didn't even know I committed Lord because you are very holy. Please cleanse me from all unrighteousness according to 1 John 1:9.

I rededicated my life back to you Jesus and ask you to be the apostle, master, and Lord over my soul.

Please destroy every idol in my life and cleanse me from every spot, wrinkle, and blemish that's on my robe that would keep me from inheriting your kingdom if you should take me home today by the power, suffering, and resurrection that Jesus accomplished while here on earth I pray in

the name of Jesus of Jesus Christ of Nazareth according to John 16:23 and I rebuke all delays from this prayer being answered by the power of the blood of Jesus amen.

Sleep

Lord Jesus we ask you as our commander of your army that's written in Joshua 5:14, for maximum strength of protection and plead your blood tonight over this prayer, our falling asleep, sleep, in between sleep, all naps, waking up, and going back to sleep.

Please forgive us of all of our sins committed on this day. Lord Jesus, we ask you to keep your hands on us while we sleep tonight. We ask you to please loose your host and legions of warring and ministering angels to protect us from all demonization, engaging in any demonic encounters, and to destroy all messengers of satan that would try to come nears us by the power and anointing your holy word, the Bible, has had on bringing your children back home from the day of its origination even until now.

Lord Jesus please protect us from all the sins of our relatives, the seven giants and decendents of Anak that's written in Numbers 13:22 & Deuteronomy 7:1, and when any and everything else satanic would try to penetrate and attack us and our families.

We ask you to block all forms of insomnia, make our reproductive body parts completely off limits, block all forms of perversion from the smallest to the highest levels of existence, preventing all torment, theft, infirmities, defilements of all kinds, anti-Christ spirit, lies, death, bondages, hurt, pain, all cancers, kidnappings of all kinds, other people's and our own soulish attacks, addictions, pride, anger, retaliation, soulish attacks of all kinds, demonic contaminations of all kinds, and fear.

We ask you to be the door keeper to the three gates and nineteen doors of our souls and we plead the blood of Jesus Christ of Nazareth over them all. Heavenly Father we pray that you would grant us sweet sleep according to Psalms 4:8 and we ask all these things according to John 16:23 and we seal this request in the name of Jesus Christ of Nazareth and pray that the power of his blood rebukes all supernatural delays amen.

Lock Down

Heavenly Father, we call you to be our Jehovah **Mekoddishkem**

We come to lock our flesh down to make sure we don't give any access to the kingdom of darkness. We put every area of carnality, the three gates and nineteen doors of our souls in us under submission to the blood of Jesus Christ of Nazareth right now in the name of Jesus.

Lord Jesus Christ of Nazareth, I ask you according to John 14:14 to supply your anointing to and destroy all evil bondages, yokes, chains, fetters, anklets, bands, all evil works roots, fruits, tentacles, and links, out of, off of, and away from me, along with any darkness, darts arrows, stings, claws spears, barbs, lies of the enemy, anything not your truth, evil imprints, evil impressions, wrong mind sets, pains, aches, false memories, and wrong mind sets.

We put the conscious and subconscious parts of our brains under the authority of Jesus Christ of Nazareth right now.

We submerge our spirits in the fire of the Holy Ghost according to Luke 3:22 so, that we can discern and attack any enemy from afar off immediately in the name of Jesus Christ we pray according to John 14:13-14. The blood of Jesus Christ of Nazareth cover and seal this entire prayer amen.

Haters

Holy Spirit please help us pray for our haters with a right spirit, we ask you to fill us with the mercy and compassion that Jesus had for his haters when they mocked him as he was dying on the cross and He yet prayed for them.

Lord Jesus your love is more powerful than anything that exist in our little world, please show our haters what their problems truly are.

Show them the enemies of their souls that's fighting the you in us and please help them to overcome them, in the meantime, we pull every demonic spirit, all forms of carnality, entities, principalities, hosts, witches, warlocks, demons, Satan himself if need be, and all devils in and on them to come down and under the subjection and authority of Jesus Christ of Nazareth and your blood Lord Jesus right now I pray according to John 16:23 amen.

We rebuke all their word curses against us, unrighteous agreements being prayed from them about us, and demons answering wrong prayers concerning us. We ask you Lord Jesus to stop them right now and all those prayers and words are cancelled and destroyed right now according to Isaiah 54:17 in the name of Jesus Christ of Nazareth and we seal this prayer in the blood of Jesus and there ain't nothing the prince of darkness nor any representative of his can do about it for all eternity in Jesus name I/we pray amen and amen.

Fight

Heavenly Father you are our Father and we need you to be **El Gibbor**.

The world is in serious trouble as you already know.

We can't catch everything in prayer with all that's going on, but right now in the name of your son Jesus, we sincerely ask you to send those 12 legions of angels that Jesus was talking about in Matthew 26:53, the arc angel Michael and his angels that's written in Revelations 12:7 and 8, and we ask that there's more angels with us than the kingdom of darkness according to 2 Kings 6:16.

We pray that they would fight for humanity against all terrorists attacks, divisions, all bullies in every school worldwide from pre-k to college, people on the verge of suicide, babies and children on the verge of being raped, molested, and killed, premature deaths, murders, rapes, homicides, car and bus accidents, plane and train accidents, boat sinking's and drownings, all types of kidnappings, all forms of sexual perversions, thefts of all kinds, addictions to drugs of all kinds, and all our generational curses in the name of Jesus Christ of Nazareth we pray according to John 16:23 and we seal this prayer in the blood of Jesus that it takes effect right now we beg you Heavenly Father amen and amen.

Keep

Heavenly Father, I ask you to be **Jehovah Nissi**, the Lord my banner. Please keep our minds and our hearts stayed on you.

Lord Jesus we ask you to keep our whole amour intact and spirit in place with you.

Lord Jesus, we ask you to restore if need be and keep our deliverances on us.

Lord Jesus, we ask you to keep your protection on and around us according to Psalm 91 1-16.

Lord Jesus, we ask you to grow your compassion and love for others and to keep us from falling from your grace in your name we pray amen.

Midnight

In the book of Acts 16:25 Paul and Silas prayed and there was a great earthquake and immediately all the doors were opened and all the prisoners bands were loosed.

We pray Heavenly Father, **El Gibbor**, for our family members near and far, our neighbors, our enemies, our co-workers, our communities, and people we all go to school and church with, people we don't know who are homeless, in hospitals, nursing homes, jails, prisons, mental hospitals, cancer treatment hospitals, VA hospitals, military hospitals, rehabilitation centers, and detention centers that are all over the world.

Lord Jesus in the Spirit realm, we ask you for a great shaking, an earthquake to open the doors of healing and deliverance, and we ask that you would come in and set us free please from all those demonic shackles that you know we need to be set free from in the name of Jesus Christ of Nazareth according to John 16:23.

We plead the blood of Jesus over this request and seal it in your blood too Jesus, in your name we pray according to John 14:13-14 amen.

Battle

Heavenly Father, we know that there is a war going on all the time for our souls. I need you to be my **El Gibbor** again for this request Lord. It is written in your word that he who wins souls is wise. We ask you to give us the boldness, prophetic anointing, and power we need to win souls to the kingdom.

We bind and loose according to Matthew 16 and 18 all fear, fear of rejection, and all spirits of opposition and division in the name of Jesus Christ of Nazareth off the people you would have us minister to. We pray that we are soul winners in the name of Jesus and that we are not ashamed of the gospel of Jesus Christ.

We pray today that your kingdom wins through all the believers and disciples of Jesus all over the world right now throughout this day and throughout the night watches in the name of Jesus we pray according to John 16:23 amen and amen.

Gifts

Heavenly Father, we ask to be our **El Rachum,** the God of compassion. Please help us all to appreciate, accept, and mature in the special gifts and talents you have called us to have and given to us in the name of Jesus.

Please enable are frenemies, family members, and especially the people we go to church and school with, to give you all the glory for what you are doing in our lives and not compare themselves to one another because we all are a part of the body of Christ.

Enable us all to stop being petty and truly rejoice and celebrate with one another, with a right spirit when you bless us and to mourn with your heart of compassion with each other when we're dealing with any kind of loss according to Romans 12:15 in the name of Jesus Christ of Nazareth amen and amen.

Blockers

Heavenly Father we pray in the name of Jesus Christ of Nazareth that you would block all of our blockers. Those in leadership positions in our churches who keep the people you want to use back from bringing you glory. Lord deliver them from only using people who's been in church for a million years with no anointing, their special groups and cliques, family members, those who were there when their church began, and those who were saved there.

We can't fight them and we're not supposed to, but we know you've called us so, we ask you to open the doors that you want us to pass through and we thank you that there's nothing the devil can do about it because like the song says, "When you say yes nobody can say no", therefore, we give you praise!

In Jesus name we pray and ask according to John 16:23 and we plead the blood of Jesus over it and we rebuke all delays that would come against it amen and amen.

Binding & Loosing

Part 2

Note: Do not say if you haven't been fasting and praying.

Heavenly Father, the Holy Spirit and I come to you right now in the name of Jesus Christ your son. For the purpose of this prayer, we ask you Lord to be the Iam that Iam as you were in the days of Moses when you used him to display your mighty power against the Egyptians.

We include in this prayer ourselves, children, parents, grandparents, neighbors, all relatives, community, our city, people we go to church with, everyone we go to school with, everyone we come into contact with, and all of our enemies known and unknown and their families, enemies, relatives, communities, cities, schools, and churches too. We lift up everyone that's in the path of danger right now, everyone that need's your divine mercy and grace right now, everyone that needs to be set free from spells and curses right now Lord that you see.

We ask you **El** Elyon to bind and loose all that were

about to say from us all in the name of your only begotten son Jesus.

Please bind and loose from us and everything that concerns us in this life the signs, symptoms, manifestations, adverse effects, stings, wrong mind sets, emotions, attacks that have come against us, in us, and in the heavens completely, the generational curses, all demonic hosts and the head of the snake of all these things listed below, the

Cain syndrome/spirit, ahiman, sheshai, talmai, jebusites, gergashite, caananite, hittites, perizzite, amorite, hivites, addiction, affinity, affliction, the curse of the bastard, ahab, jezebel, antichrist, lucifer, backsliding, apathy, balaam, belial, carnality, competition, deaf and dumb, confusion, depression, desolation, rebellion, death, divination, fear and torment, idolatry, jealousy and envy, judas, korah, madness and mental illness, murder, oppression, perversion, pride, poverty and financial curses, rebellion, rejection, religion, self-righteousness, sabotage, seduction, shame, adultery, fornication, lying, bitterness and the poison effects of it, suspicion, tradition, unclean spirits, vexation spirits in the name of Jesus Christ of Nazareth and please send them straight to the pit of hell and we place the blood of the Lord Jesus Christ of Nazareth between us right now throughout this day, throughout the night and early morning watch hours, even until our full deliverances come according to your time table.

Lord Jesus my commander, we ask you to loose

these things from our feelings, emotions, our spirits, our tongues, mouths, our soul, our reproductive organs, our witness for you wherever we go, our fingers, eyes, ears, nose, throat, chest, our coming and going, our thinking patterns, our homes, the deep places of our hearts, our hormones and chemical balances in our bodies.

Please fill us and loose into each of us your submission, integrity, purpose, timing of the Lord, the heart of a servant, humility, apostolic anointing, wisdom, peace, truth, prophetic intercession, self-control, righteousness, love, boldness, sound mind, hope, maturity, liberty, protection, forgiveness, conviction of the Holy Spirit, holiness, the will of God, God-and Christ-centeredness, deliverance, discerning of spirits, obedience, loyalty, fear of God and covenant, giving anointing, joy, sense of significance, healing balm of Gilead, fruit of the spirit, discipline, expedience, fellowship, unity, harmony, meekness, moderation, purity of heart, true and pure worship, the manifestation of the gifts of the spirit, anointing of Elijah, anointing Jehu, divine visitations, soul-winning, power, spiritual mindedness, courage, repentance, satisfaction, celebration, kindness, brotherly love, godliness, fire of the Lord, terror of the Lord,

breaking the curse of whoredom, control to be torn down and ripped to shreds, break chains and soulish ties from current and past generations, order the veils of curses, order, trustworthiness, prosperity, liberality in giving, abundant life, true humility, compliance, fasting, revelation of the hidden secrets of the heart, prayer, the wrath of God (Ezekiel 13: 11-15) please in the name of Jesus Christ of Nazareth and we plead the blood of Jesus over this entire prayer and process and seal it in the blood of Jesus Christ of Nazareth in your name we pray according to John 16:23 amen.

Index

Fighting Words

<u>Psalms 91: 1-16</u>

He that dwelleth in the secret place of the most High shall abide under the shadow of the Almighty.

2 I will say of the LORD, He is my refuge and my fortress: my God; in him will I trust.

3 Surely he shall deliver thee from the snare of the fowler, and from the noisome pestilence.

4 He shall cover thee with his feathers, and under his wings shalt thou trust: his truth shall be thy shield and buckler.

5 Thou shalt not be afraid for the terror by night; nor for the arrow that flieth by day;

6 Nor for the pestilence that walketh in darkness; nor for the destruction that wasteth at noonday.

7 A thousand shall fall at thy side, and ten thousand at thy right hand; but it shall not come nigh thee.

⁸ Only with thine eyes shalt thou behold and see the reward of the wicked.

⁹ Because thou hast made the LORD, which is my refuge, even the most High, thy habitation;

¹⁰ There shall no evil befall thee, neither shall any plague come nigh thy dwelling.

¹¹ For he shall give his angels charge over thee, to keep thee in all thy ways.

¹² They shall bear thee up in their hands, lest thou dash thy foot against a stone.

¹³ Thou shalt tread upon the lion and adder: the young lion and the dragon shalt thou trample under feet.

¹⁴ Because he hath set his love upon me, therefore will I deliver him: I will set him on high, because he hath known my name.

¹⁵ He shall call upon me, and I will answer him: I will be with him in trouble; I will deliver him, and honour him.

¹⁶ With long life will I satisfy him, and shew him my salvation.

Psalm 23

The LORD is my shepherd; I shall not want.

² He maketh me to lie down in green pastures: he leadeth me beside the still waters.

3 He restoreth my soul: he leadeth me in the paths of righteousness for his name's sake.

4 Yea, though I walk through the valley of the shadow of death, I will fear no evil: for thou art with me; thy rod and thy staff they comfort me.

5 Thou preparest a table before me in the presence of mine enemies: thou anointest my head with oil; my cup runneth over.

6 Surely goodness and mercy shall follow me all the days of my life: and I will dwell in the house of the LORD forever.

Job 1:10

Hast not thou made an hedge about him, and about his house, and about all that he hath on every side? thou hast blessed the work of his hands, and his substance is increased in the land.

Exodus 12:13

And the blood shall be to you for a token upon the houses where ye are: and when I see the blood, I will pass over you, and the plague shall not be upon you to destroy you, when I smite the land of Egypt.

Against Works of the Flesh

Mark 7:21 & 22

For from within, out of the heart of men, proceed evil thoughts, adulteries, fornications, murders, Thefts, covetousness, wickedness, deceit, lasciviousness, an evil eye, blasphemy, pride, foolishness:

Ephesians 4:31

Let all bitterness, and wrath, and anger, and clamour, and evil speaking, be put away from you, with all malice:

1 Corinthians 6:9 & 10

Know ye not that the unrighteous shall not inherit the kingdom of God? Be not deceived: neither fornicators, nor idolaters, nor adulterers, nor effeminate, nor abusers of themselves with mankind, nor thieves, nor covetous, nor drunkards, nor revilers, nor extortioners, shall inherit the kingdom of God.

Galatians 5: 19, 20, & 21

Now the works of the flesh are manifest, which are these; Adultery, fornication, uncleanness, lasciviousness, Idolatry, witchcraft, hatred, variance, emulations, wrath, strife, seditions, heresies,

21 Envying's, murders, drunkenness, reveling, and such like: of the which I tell you before, as I have also told you in time past, that they which do such things shall not inherit the kingdom of God.

2 Timothy 3:2-5

2 For men shall be lovers of their own selves, covetous, boasters, proud, blasphemers, disobedient to parents, unthankful, unholy,

3 Without natural affection, trucebreakers, false accusers, incontinent, fierce, despisers of those that are good,

4 Traitors, heady, high-minded, lovers of pleasures more than lovers of God;

5 Having a form of godliness, but denying the power thereof: from such turn away.

Romans 1:29-32

Being filled with all unrighteousness, fornication,

wickedness, covetousness, maliciousness; full of envy, murder, debate, deceit, malignity; whisperers,

30 Backbiters, haters of God, despiteful, proud, boasters, inventors of evil things, disobedient to parents,31 Without understanding, covenant breakers, without natural affection, implacable, unmerciful:32 Who knowing the judgment of God, that they which commit such things are worthy of death, not only do the same, but have pleasure in them that do them.

Help & Healing

Psalm 121:1-8

I will lift up mine eyes unto the hills, from whence cometh my help.

2 My help cometh from the LORD, which made heaven and earth.

3 He will not suffer thy foot to be moved: he that keepeth thee will not slumber.

4 Behold, he that keepeth Israel shall neither slumber nor sleep.

5 The LORD is thy keeper: the LORD is thy shade upon thy right hand.

6 The sun shall not smite thee by day, nor the moon by night.

7 The LORD shall preserve thee from all evil: he shall preserve thy soul.

8 The LORD shall preserve thy going out and thy coming in from this time forth, and even for evermore.

Exodus 15:26

And said, If thou wilt diligently hearken to the voice of the LORD thy God, and wilt do that which is right in his sight, and wilt give ear to his commandments, and keep all his statutes, I will put none of these diseases upon thee, which I have brought upon the Egyptians: for I am the LORD that healeth thee.

Jude 1:20-21

But ye, beloved, building up yourselves on your most holy faith, praying in the Holy Ghost, Keep yourselves in the love of God, looking for the mercy of our Lord Jesus Christ unto eternal life.

Galatians 5:22-24

But the fruit of the Spirit is love, joy, peace, longsuffering, gentleness, goodness, faith,[23] Meekness, temperance: against such there is no law.[24] And they that are Christ's have crucified the flesh with the affections and lusts.

Names of God

Elohay Mishpat - God Of Justice

Elohay Selichot - God Of Forgiveness

Elohay Mauzi - God Of My Strength

Elohay Tehilati - God Of My Praise

Elohay Yishi - God Of My Salvation

El Rachum- The God of compassion

El Channun- The gracious God

El Gibbor-Mighty God

El Shaddai - Lord God Almighty

El Elyon - The Most High God

Adonai - Lord, Master

Yahweh - Lord, Jehovah

Jehovah Nissi - The Lord My Banner)

Jehovah-Raah - The Lord My Shepherd)

Jehovah Rapha -The Lord That Heals)

Jehovah Shammah - The Lord Is There)

Jehovah Tsidkenu - The Lord Our Righteousness

Jehovah Mekoddishkem - The Lord Who Sanctifies You

El Olam- The Everlasting God)

Elohim - God

Qanna - Jealous

Jehovah Jireh - Lord Will Provide

Jehovah Shalom - The Lord Is Peace

Jehovah Sabaoth - The Lord of Hosts

Angels and Armies 2 Call

Revelation 12:7-8, "And there was war in heaven, **Michael and his angels waging war with the dragon.** The dragon and his angels waged war, 8 and they were not strong enough, and there was no longer a place found for thcm in heaven."

Gabriel means "man of God." He appears to be one who carries messages.

Revelation 19:14 King James Version (KJV)

14 And **the armies which were in heaven** followed him upon white horses, clothed in fine linen, white and clean.

Joshua 5:14

"Neither," he replied, "but as **commander of the army of the LORD** I have now come." Then Joshua fell facedown to the ground in reverence, and asked him, "What message does my Lord have for his servant?"

Matthew 26:53

Do you think that I cannot appeal to my Father, and he will at once send me **more than twelve legions of angels**?